THUNGACHI

THUNGACHI

POEMS BY

FRANCINE SIMON

UHLANGA

2017

Thungachi
© Francine Simon, 2017, all rights reserved

Published in Cape Town, South Africa by uHlanga in 2017
UHLANGAPRESS.CO.ZA

Distributed outside South Africa by African Books Collective
africanbookscollective.com

ISBN: 978-0-620-73507-0

Edited by Nick Mulgrew
Cover by Nick Mulgrew

Proofread by Jennifer Jacobs

The body text of this book is set in Garamond Premier Pro 11PT on 16PT

Earlier versions of some of the poems in this book originally appeared in the
following literary journals, websites and anthologies: *New Coin*, *New Contrast*,
Aerodrome, *BooksLIVE*, and *Type/Cast*. The author would like to thank the editors
of these publications, as well as the editors of the Sol Plaatje/European Union
Award for publishing some of these poems in their anthologies
in 2012, 2014, and 2015.

ACKNOWLEDGEMENTS

I would like to thank my family, immediate and extended, for helping me to understand/misunderstand us. Thank you to my mother and father. This was not your plan for me but you supported me anyway. Thank you to my sister for keeping an eye on me and being so strong. I could not have written this without all of you.

To Professor Sally-Ann Murray, thank you so much. If it were not for you, I would not be where I am. You were not just my mentor but to me you were my champion.

Thank you to my editor, Nick. You are one of the hardest workers I know and I can't thank you enough for taking such great care of these poems. It means so much to me. You made this an amazing experience.

To my two closest friends, what can I say? You have had such impact on my life. You watched the poems as they grew and loved them. That in itself gave me joy and confidence.

Thank you to Christoph, you are my partner and my immeasurable support. The small and big ways that you helped me mean everything to me still. Ego amo te.

—F.S.

C O N T E N T S

I

NAMING PLACES

When they came on the boats
one name was Sing(h).
The other, said and sung
 – lost.

Both left in faith
expecting us not
to come back.

Nair (Nayar).
Gabriel. Pillai. Placed here,
those names still carry but
we cannot feel them.

And since we don't know
my father's family
we are the last of the Simons.

Nothing left for his daughters
but to be girls.

DHOLL

You will receive
    rations as follows:
        Dholl – 2 lbs per month,
        Salt Fish – 2 lbs per month,
        Ghee or oil – 1 lb per month,
        Salt – 1 lb per month.

Acting Protector of Immigrants
"Notice to Coolies Intending to Emigrate to Natal, 17 August 1874"

We sit together
at a table smoking

pickled words
small oval leaves

fall never fitting
into a sentence.

Green shirt
one square button

it does not suit him
yet his arms come faster

'til I have a face
with four fingers
and an itch of hair
wisps loose.

Lit match, he stops
draws from the well:

My lover never called me Dholl.

I look up, one eye
sideways to the sun.

TAMIL FAMILIARS

Grandmother used
to warn me not to whistle:
I'd call the snakes.

She forbad me
to sleep with my hair open:
I'd wake up looking like a pichachi,
gone to hell and back.

She said not to eat
out of the pot or it would rain
on my wedding day.

I did and I do.

My mother tells me not to
pick from the curry-leaf tree
when it's that time of month.
It will die, she says.

Funny. It hasn't died yet.
And I never give a thought
to my wedding.

Tea

At home, we have no tea tray.

Tea is served in each hand   one by one   cup balanced on saucer

everything   all in   already added.

No "Milk and sugar?"

Tea is simply served,

though it must be brought to the guest properly

accompanied by Marie biscuits or Eet-sum-mors.

Tea is my job. I know it well.

my godfather	–	tea black, two sugars
my aunt	–	tea (hot milk!) and quarter sugar
my father	–	tea double sugared, two sugars boiled:

he takes his tea with the bag in milk, then more boiled water added after. He told me his grandfather warmed the cups with hot water before making tea, which apparently is the proper way.

He never said which grandfather, which side.
Was it his father?   I don't know
I don't know   why I wonder about that.

I take tea but never drink it.
You can always find a cold cup
and know it's me.

LATE

Girl of seven when I saw the skeleton.
Afternoon at the beach across from the hospital,
a ghost, paled by the sun.

My father sat on the breaker line
waiting for a wave. A she-whale   the elephant bones
of a baby cupped beneath her spine.

Head to tail   mother and calf   beached
touch the baby, skull white as an unlit wick.

Then my father was calling, board in hand, and I ran,
presented him with a half-shell story. Asked him
if lady whales had a hospital and if their husbands

                                        picked   clean.   I stretched to

were allowed to visit. Maybe, he said. She could have been waiting

for her husband. Maybe when I swam   he said

I'd hear the deep, long echo the man-whale sang, promising his mate

never to be late.

GATHERING

Everything gathers dust.
I learnt that from my mother
while she wiped every surface,
metal frames, paper, wood.

But she doesn't know everything about
dust. The box of rippled photos
under my desk, stolen
so that they can breathe.

She guards the others.
Obituaries frame our walls:

Ma, Ma two,
little sister. Family portrait.
Woman in that brown dress,
beaded velvet, long sleeves.
We never wear brown
but she pictures really well
holding a baby. Twice.

All are broken clocks
and candle stumps.
Dust, watching
in a settlement.

II

Pp

pakka   ADJ.
She's not a pakka Indian

patha   N.
Made from the leaves of the madumbi plant

paneer   N.
She likes to eat paneer but

porridge-prayers   N.
For the Mother Goddess... may be accompanied
by the sacrifice of:
goat or ~~domestic~~ running fowl

poli   N.
"How she can make poli at Diwali time!"   1

Parvati   N.
Likes guava, running fowl and puri-path   2

pulled up   ADJ.
I don't know what she was pulled up for

parcel   N.
when I said "Did Danny come with my
parcel?" she turned her head to her books

pottemāri   N.
I closed the door telling you she's a pottemāri   3

paining   PART.
"Mummy, mummy! My eye's paining!"

put eyes   V. PHR.
she said you look so beautiful; when you go
home, you must turn salt or

pig-sty   N.
you'll get a pig-sty   4

peri-vai   N.
"Don't be a peri-vai! You got a big mouth."

put chillies   V. PHR.
"I'll put chillies in your eyes for you!"   5

pull out   V.
can you really pull out from

pichachi   N.
She-demon?   6

Rati

Ja, I know the story about how I was made. Brahma created everyone different and Kama came from his mind. No one really gets that actually he's the god of love. He rides this mountain parrot. I know, right? But anyway, one of the ten kings, Daksha, was supposed to give him a wife. Maybe he owed Brahma a favour for making him or something. And Kama was supposed to spread love or some shit in the world but he went against that and shot flower-arrows at Brahma and Daksha and the other guys. They fall in love with Brahma's daughter and then they get super embarrassed. So embarrassed that they sweat. From Daksha's sweat, I came. I guess. I mean, do you just sweat and that becomes a person? I ride a parrot too but, like, a parrot made out of smaller women. I have a sword which is way better than Kama's sugarcane bow. You probably know me from that one position in *Kama Sutra* called "Rati's noose" or the painting of me and Kama hooking up on a mat with headless pichachi standing on us? It's really not like Song of Songs. It was just three sips of honey and blood for three nights with me and her head moving around on the floor. He has his hands in my hair and I'm his complex hole, I–

Bride

1 I am putting on my wedding
   dress, clipping
   white hooks

   Dad comes after
   the Nikah, tells me   I'm married
   shouldn't keep from

   meeting my husband
   now

   ten tables set   I am ready
   with the tea tray
   between one Indian Moon moth

   and boiled veil
   milk   cups
   warmed

   his name begins with a lingual bone
   dressed in an eggshell suit
   bent double by mother

   two sugar   hot water
   extra milk

   he waits on a soft
   serve chaise

11   Your kitchen had a strong white breath.
      Fixed with pots, it was husband and wife
      a   pipe
      a   kettle
      (broken) so it's second element.

      You are a man of no shape,
      especially in the early morning –
      bat   neck
      cow   feet
      a spiracle love of pools.

      She takes the teabag out her cup
      squeezes it, leaves it
      on the windowsill to age –
      soft   as skin
      dark   as cum.

      Now she is with me.

      We picnic often.

      You always thought
      you knew so much.

NANNI-MA

I think of sex and only
sex since he
became my neighbour

in the flat next door.
And you, in the garden outside,
a goat named Ma.

He adores you,
milks you in the early hours
for his morning porridge.

I watch in my nightie,
confused by hands
on your soft, uddery skin.

It reminds me of nights
he touched me,
not an old skinned goat.

My lips turning half pages,
exposing pink marrow
bones for him to lick.

But you I would never wear
for a thick waistcoat.
I'd miss your fat eyes

in my doorway at night
asking to eat from
my chilli tree.

#9

I hang like a
harp under sand
one eye softened
like a fringed patina
would you swim
            inside?
find a body

length and breath
so flashing
and old

                                                            removing
could you   cane knives
        live under   and sand of
            my spine then   our Kala Pani
clean your nails   *or*

Trial and error

Knead me down
divide me thirty
palms of dough
your fingers sting
yet you know:
take your time

lay me turn
me with fingertips
use the curl of your hands
making me
a circle.

Each time you rolled
and pressed
I grew more round
each one of me
ready to be
pan-oiled

then suddenly stop
you come to
a   standstill

oh

my mother never told me
it comes with   practice.

I never told you   either.

III

KREUZIGEN

he came to the meeting of towels
as if he had been given Viva's signet ring
she met him there
they sat at the tabernacle
it was not gold
but he put rings on her eyebrow

despite her age or fight
despite his mouth on Devi or Kali or some other form
despite the end of godhood

there was not a meeting after this
– only her hair falling into his eyes
on *soilsheen nights*

VETALA-PACHISI

(1987)

and when you lit that candle
it was hard enough to ask so instead you burned

Hail Marys into your hands. Black dot
on your forehead. Rice mouse in your teeth.

(1943)

she knew that he watched
her steps when they rippled
like river waves.

But then she caught his eye.
He looked away. No mouth.
He was much too old either way.

(2012)

it has been many years

since   *I came back here*
dead   *zoo*   *vetala*

head   *leopard with his catch*
feet   *pool of plastic blood*

I always thought

              looking around
he was above me

but the museum is inside

They say a sorcerer
once asked King Vikramaditya
to capture a vetala who lived in a tree
that stood in the middle of a crematorium.

The only way to do that was by keeping silent.

But each time the king caught the ghost
the ghost would enchant the king
with a story that ended
with a question.

No matter how much he tried
the king found himself
unable to resist giving
an answer.

SHEEP'S HEAD

Because of my aunt I have grown so fat,
even fox terriers smell like butter bread
and garden birds of smoked, dried duck.

She feeds me tripe and beans,
trotters and gram dhall. "Your favourite!
Dish, dish. Don' worry, girl."

Eat eat eat. It would be Christmas soon,
I thought, and she'd buy sheep's head to cook.
How I hated those dull, blunt eyes

offered to me like onyx.
"One day maybe she'll talk but,"
I heard her say to my mother.

IV

PRESENT CONTINUOUS

to walk up a red staircase
my skins spilt   gathering down
I cannot even coil them
not in   glass displays
my face is nature-science pink
I am wearing   a pink jacket
pink   pants

          I find Ma at the sewing museum
          and cry that I don't have skin
she wants to smile   say I don't need it
          while she pulls from cat-animals
          stitches hides onto each of my bones
I do not fall asleep with her fingers on me

you are drawing a diagram
an upside-down vase in the back-lined book you

          my boy cousins visit
                    throwing
          at the monkeys   laughing

I am only watching from my scooter
from my mouth   lizard oranges come
trees shake females   screaming down
                    baring cunts

my cousin catches a mother
          hitting her with a stone
and her child bent on the tarmac
          soft body flat

          after three days she sits there
                    as her baby moulds
          she touches his head his feet
                    my parents leave her be

show a small egg travelling down   you say
that it will break up become blood   this will
happen to me
it will come once a month   but not yet
I'm still too young

I cover my eyes as I am told and when:
          her skin intrigues me
curled hair cannot cover her chest
          those lips and window
          I do not understand their sweat

I press my hand into leather couch
don't eat enough that night
I croak too

later my throat is too thin
a R5 coin is trying to fall
will I wake up screaming in Ma's arms

I knee down   chillies rubbed in my eyes
this inner room   burns
I don't mean it   was it so bad
I say   blurred Hail Marys
I beg   it's dark please
I promise   no I won't again

          splash toilet water into my eyes
          wait on cut-cross knees

          I swat between the cross
          it is cold   I am cold
          hangers take off my clothes
          fingers put on my wood slate
          just inside   red lock
          a golden calf slips under door

          Little fish! Little fish!
               Can you swim on land?
          Can you swim freestyle as fast as you can?

CHAIR BEARS

before the cupboard you were the pink ring I smelt
who liked to
tumble with me in the grass
push each other down in the pool

that Saturday Tazos and wet bangs bring us inside
me asking where are the scissors?
you lead me to the Singer pull them from the under-box

we cut our dresses down the middle
I see chipboard bed base our tiled backs begin to listen
my hands are Gabriel-cold you feel like barracuda tongues
I try hold your wrists
no one is in the house

in the cupboard you eat raw chicken breast
I join you

V

Promise

BYE

"Charlie,   Charlie!"

I have a bird   My coat is heavy   I am afraid of you

R5 for taxi   I only want your hand   Penicillin's in my body

Put white bread   Superglued back
on my lap   to right boot

"I'll text you just now   Or you can just tell me tomorrow."

House

he comes down
the street shouting
words in pidgin
about running fowls
aunty Tucky called for him
she repeats aunty's words
kneeling for the window
suede print down her shins

Yard

s w e e p i n g
still in the box
without using Fs and Bs
or making eyes
like y'oll
two plaits
Kristoff dress
s w e e p i n g

Tree

I sat on the guava tree
that topi head comes when
early morning fingers move
plastic washing pegs
a fourth time this month

Rombu unbu

I say mi amor.

I think I should say
rombu unbu. But
I do not know the words

so I close my eyes.

I wish for rabbits' whiskers
as his lips grow
a tongue touching

a stitch for unlearnt thunee.

His beard makes
small holes in me,
drawing blood.

r o m b u   u n b u

Words ghost my lips
in a split second that stirs
my mother tongue.

Indigo dogfire writer

While you were smo king I wat ched,

tra cing over my note book. The time
and date were speech les s and I want
ed to wrap that up, shu f fle it away in
a jack of clubs. I wrote down your na
me amongst others with three hearts be
side it, and one diamond. I had twen
ty talents. You read and smoked with
out looking up, and your glasses neve
r seemed to slip down as you ashed or
turned a page I went back to my work.
Only ten talents left. Ten 10 10 10 10
the others smo   king.

VI

CREATURE

if I could put you on
my belly like an otter
does a crab

and crack you open
with a smooth
dark stone

I would eat you
your grey flesh raw
as a split dawn clam

I would lap up
your small smile
and lick your lips

your coral entrails
dripping from my arms
without a word

LITTLE HOUSE

We say little.
Instead, we build
this house thick

as risen dough, tongue-
words stuck in the batter.

The roof of a mouth
caves in in the wind,
floor lettered in sounds

nothing but whimpers.

Nothing here,
only dust

on our words in want
of a wiping hand.

#6

– please – it's been six days since I saw your
skin. I was dog. You were cat. We
were different but why? I hated a rough tongue
in my mouth but you held my face on Monday.

– what do you want? – you unhinged my jaw
like I was eating your whole liver and each of
your plum kidneys.

– here – I said. I was telling you – cut my
palms – split them down to ten without tails.

So I showed you my gōngxi hands. Again,
again, when I dried you like gander, rabbit
buck and pen.

– could you be any more annoying – I took
that down, peeling in my absolution, and fresh
like salt, swayed in
place where your chest had been. – I don't like
girls, Fran –

SHRIVE

it was not known as Shrove Tuesday yet
my fat I made into 16 pancakes using 2 eggs
300 ml milk
100g flour
we ate all the best things in the house
until your stomach bloated like a week

you began getting ready for Mass the same way
praying to St. Anne
piercing yours and my feet with needles
putting kajal as novena
I demand of you   three wet threes
give me glass   cut your tongue with tumbler
cough blood into my blood

I use a funnel to open food into your mouth
sewing in lips to make you Rati's daughter

you struggle with lip noises every now and then

but as I was mustard yellow once
I knew the right tumbler

and now Uncle Johnny's glass is a soft reminder
for our thighs

SPUR

She wears a red dot and her hair middle-parted
We sit together at Tallahassee Spur
Buy-one-get-one-free waffles
She licks the knife from the ice cream cut
the round edge put to the side
cream dries from a half drop on the table
I want to go back with you she says
to the room with two doors
and you holding the Bible in one hand
It's the end of the month
she has no place to go
Her eyelids begin to droop
she finishes
you know I'm good at
dropping things
on the floor

VII

WINDOW

No one knows how many dead crocodiles are here.
The frame sees black boxes of fish forgotten in the airport.
I scramble any kind of pronoun for them.
The trembling carpet watches me when I eat the runway
and subdivide dusty puns from bottled glass.
Waiting for my crocodile's body to arrive. I paid black money for him.

Lucky, his eyes were fresh and juicy. I was famished.
His taste was mine; everything made sense when I sucked on his bones.
In the window, crocodile babies all wear white idioms.

At that window, I learnt to dress the same without phrase.
And I would love those scaly babies – but reptiles are always out to get me.
You know how little boys can be.

\# 8

There is a place in our community we call the fountain.
I meet you there on Thursdays because I only work at three
and we roll ourselves in the water like Cape fur seals.

Kali

Once I met Passio

my tongue couldn't worm a y
he liked my ankle bells
then he said
Kali
(etc.)

his hand already to my mouth.

I woke like a candle
straddled between two fish.

His voice the sound
of my name

Kali. Kali!

How could I know him?

Later he walked me to church
belly to hand to skirt.

I told him. I loved him.
He kept my lion tail.

Betel-nut

I am dark but
they say I'm bluffing.
I snack on tamarind seeds

sucking while Mom makes brinjal.
Black tongue, mangrove mud   between my toes.
She's not like us but.

This is why I am not like them.
I wouldn't say *that*,
but I would say that

when she tells me all about climbing
jackfruit trees at aunty's house, she calls me
girl, losing my name.

Lately, I try out their voice: oiyoh, but it's so hard eh!
She, she don't fright for nothing.
She don't know nothing too.

It's ayyo when I check
my brand new dictionary,
a book to mark bed-made words.

The Indians, they put eyes on me except
when I go to Chatsworth
then my sentences end but.

What happened to my degree?
That's what I wonder anyway,
spitting betel-nuts, white husk.

NOTES ON POEMS

Naming places: agricultural clans, matriarchy, your child will not inherit your name

Dholl: the academic community is small, lover as sustenance, Douglas Livingstone

Tamil familiars: grandmother as character, mother as person, good Indian wives, it's probably going to rain in Durban anyway

Tea: relative fact, you have to know when you have to pull it back out

Late: yang, child-consciousness, conscious that I am not a child, Thursday mornings for medication, illegitimate children, outnumbered by women

Gathering: yin, her eyes are closed in the one on the wall, T-shirt, velvet dress, baptism gowns

Pp: Rajend Mesthrie, half-me, half-sister, surnames as food, *Harry Potter*, multi-identitied goddesses

Rati: god as young adult, girl on top, legs wrapped around, sounds a bit mean to the woman, to the man, I'm not sure?

Bride: *the men are back!*, a falling out, the same degrees, a graphic designer, the cousins at the doorway, peeling off a bunch of hundreds

Nanni-ma: Bob Marley, otherwise self-explanatory

#9: oarfish found dead on the shore, the True Indians, derivatives, dark waters

Trial and error: roti, things you're afraid to do, but something you're never sure you can master

Kreuzigen: Stations of the Cross, looser than loosely, someone like Shiva

Vetala-pachisi: soulmate-seeking, intercession, grandparents meeting at a class, the asthmatic instructor, ballroom dancing champions, *this is a man you are a child*; Durban Natural Science Museum, a lineage, *I will always be a king but I'll never have a people*

Sheep's head: *Angela's Ashes*, what they would do without their feet

Present continuous: night terrors, Riverside, trying to pick my skin up, the museum with the sewing machine, she stitches me back together, strong swimmers

chair bears: parents concerned about Pokemon, letters to the editor, possession

Promise: ouija, Bloody Mary, *Candyman*, *American Horror Story*, antibiotics, oachkatzlschwoaf

House Yard Tree: a crush on the poultry man in Chatsworth

Rombu unbu: not using your ancestral tongue, *I don't remember saying that*, translation, *does it really mean that?*

Indigo dogfire writer: Harry Potter playing thunee, two Indian guys in Metallica T-shirts, I smoked for a long time, the ten talents

Creature: there are twins who are exceptionally brilliant, he was a short story writer, he now writes erotica, cocaine

Little house: the ability to only whimper

#6: dog meat and soup at the cafeteria, I'm pretty sure I went on a date with her but I didn't know it was a date

Shrive: a figure of physical love, diamonds in the tumblers

Spur: Buffalo wings, I went back for my birthday last year, crumbed mushrooms, Somerset Mall

Window: newspaper clippings photocopied onto blank pages, baby crocodiles were airmailed to SA and arrived dead

#8: "Primal Scene", the McDonald's at Wanda Plaza, Benji at the aquarium

Kali: ankle bells were authenticity, humans into animals, two fish is from the two fish and five loaves, she woke like a candle

Betel-nut: bluffing, coconuts, Model-C, my mother calls me girl still

POETRY FOR THE PEOPLE

AVAILABLE NOW:

Modern Rasputin by Rosa Lyster

Prunings by Helen Moffett

Questions for the Sea by Stephen Symons

Failing Maths and My Other Crimes by Thabo Jijana
WINNER OF THE 2016 INGRID JONKER PRIZE FOR POETRY

Matric Rage by Genna Gardini
COMMENDED FOR THE 2016 INGRID JONKER PRIZE FOR POETRY

the myth of this is that we're all in this together by Nick Mulgrew

COMING IN 2017:

Collective Amnesia by Koleka Putuma

AVAILABLE FROM GOOD BOOKSTORES IN SOUTH AFRICA
& ELSEWHERE FROM THE AFRICAN BOOKS COLLECTIVE,
IN PRINT AND DIGITAL

UHLANGAPRESS.CO.ZA

Printed in the United States
By Bookmasters